21st Century Junior Library

WORKING ON A FARM

by Katie Marsico

CHERRY LAKE PUBLISHING * ANN ARBOR, MICHIGAN

CHERRY LAKE
Publishing

Published in the United States of America by Cherry Lake Publishing
Ann Arbor, Michigan
www.cherrylakepublishing.com

Content Adviser: Sharon Castle, PhD, Associate Professor of Elementary Social Studies,
George Mason University, Fairfax, Virginia

Reading Consultant: Cecilia Minden-Cupp, PhD, Literacy Specialist and Author

Photo Credits: Cover and page 4, ©iStockphoto.com/onepony; page 6, ©Jim West/Alamy;
cover and page 8, ©iStockphoto.com/tmcnem; page 10, ©Nitipong Ballapavanich, used under
license from Shutterstock, Inc.; cover and page 12, ©iStockphoto.com/Nnehring, page 14,
©iStockphoto.com/genekrebs; page 16, ©iStockphoto.com/Tootles; cover and page 18, page 20,
©Jim West/Alamy

LIBRARY OF CONGRESS CATALOGING-IN-PUBLICATION DATA
Marsico, Katie, 1980–
Working on a farm / by Katie Marsico.
    p. cm.
Includes index.
ISBN-13: 978-1-60279-271-5
ISBN-10: 1-60279-271-2
1. Agriculture—Juvenile literature. 2. Farms—Juvenile literature.
3. Farmers—Juvenile literature. 4. Agricultural laborers—Juvenile
literature. I. Title.
S519.M26 2009
630.023—dc22   2008007250

Cherry Lake Publishing would like to acknowledge the work of
The Partnership for 21st Century Skills.
Please visit www.21stcenturyskills.org for more information.

CONTENTS

Some farmers raise cows.

What Is a Farm?

Do you hear a low mooing sound? Look around you. Cows are everywhere! You are on a farm.

A farmer raises animals or grows plants. Both are used to make **products** you need every day. There are different types of farms. There are also different workers on a farm. Farmers are just one example.

A worker feeds goats on a farm.

Have you ever visited a farm? You probably saw a lot of busy workers. Everyone works together to take care of the plants and animals. Let's take a look at some farm workers.

Look!

Many products in your home come from farms. Look in your kitchen. Can you find five items that farm workers helped to make or grow? Hint: Milk, eggs, and bread are a few examples.

Farm workers use tractors to pull machines for planting crops.

Farm Workers

Farmers who raise plants have many important jobs. They make sure seeds are planted at just the right time. They **harvest** the **crops** that are finished growing.

Farmers who raise animals must take good care of them. They make sure that the animals get enough food and water. They must keep the animals healthy.

Many farmers use machines to milk their cows.

Some farmers use machines to get the soil ready for planting. Other farmers own machines that milk cows. Who makes sure the machines work the right way? **Mechanics** often do this job. These workers fix farm machines that break down.

Who else do farmers work with? Some farmers hire **veterinarians**. A veterinarian is an animal doctor. She helps keep the farm animals healthy.

Laborers work hard to harvest crops.

Farmers also work with experts who look at the soil. These experts study how plants are growing. They also give farmers advice about what will make plants grow better.

Running a farm is a big job. This is why farmers hire **laborers**. Some laborers help plant seeds or harvest crops. Others load trucks when it is time for animals or crops to leave the farm.

Some farmers sell their fruits and vegetables at farmer's markets.

Where do the animals and crops go? Food factories and grocery stores buy them. They use them to create items that you buy when you go shopping.

Farmers buy things from stores that sell farm supplies. They need food for the animals and seeds to grow plants.

Wheat is loaded onto a truck at harvest time.

Who brings these supplies to farmers? This is usually a truck driver's job. Truck drivers also take the crops and animals from the farm to the people who buy them. Truck drivers bring the foods and other products to the stores you shop in, too.

Ask Questions!

Are there any farms in your area? If so, call and ask if you can visit one of them. Ask about the different jobs on each farm. Maybe you will decide that you want one of these jobs someday!

Some people enjoy working with animals.

Do You Want to Work on a Farm?

Would you like to work on a farm? It is not too early to start planning ahead! Talk to workers the next time you visit a farm. Find out why they chose their jobs. Ask what they like best about their jobs.

Some farm workers are good with animals. Others enjoy raising plants. How can you get ready for a job on a farm?

Working in a garden can help you decide if you might like farm work.

You can spend time working in a garden. Does your family have pets? Help take good care of them. Maybe you can help friends or neighbors take care of their pets, too.

A farm can be a great place to work. Learn as much as you can now. Maybe you will decide that a farm job is right for you!

Create!

Want to get some practice growing plants? Ask your parents if you can start your own small garden. Make a list of all the plants you want to include. Then plant some seeds. Take good care of them and watch them grow.

GLOSSARY

crops (KRAHPS) plants that farmers grow to be eaten or used in other products

harvest (HAR-vest) to gather crops on a farm

laborers (LAY-bur-urz) workers who help farmers with chores such as harvesting crops and loading animals onto trucks

mechanics (meh-KAH-niks) workers who fix machines that are used on a farm

products (PRAH-dukts) foods or other items that are created using a process

veterinarians (veh-teh-ruh-NER-ee-uhnz) doctors who help keep farmers' animals healthy

FIND OUT MORE

BOOKS

Kalman, Bobbie. *Veterinarians Help Keep Animals Healthy*. New York: Crabtree Publishing Company, 2005.

Sirett, Dawn. *Farmer for a Day*. New York: DK Publishing, 2004.

WEB SITES

American Veterinary Medical Association— Animated Journeys: About Veterinarians
www.avma.org/careforanimals/ animatedjourneys/aboutvets/ aboutvetsfl.asp
Read about veterinarians and the different jobs they do

U.S. Department of Labor—Bureau of Labor Statistics (Farmer)
www.bls.gov/k12/nature03.htm
Learn more about what farmers do and how you can prepare to be a farmer

INDEX

ABOUT THE AUTHOR

Katie Marsico is the author of more than 30 children's books. She lives in Elmhurst, Illinois, with her husband and two children. She would especially like to thank the staff at the Illinois Farm Bureau for helping her research this title.